Adventure SPORTS

HIKING

Stephanie Turnbull

A$^+$
Smart Apple Media

Published by Smart Apple Media, an imprint of Black Rabbit Books
P.O. Box 3263, Mankato, Minnesota, 56002
www.blackrabbitbooks.com

Printed in the United States of America, at Corporate Graphics
in North Mankato, Minnesota.

Designed and illustrated by Guy Callaby
Edited by Mary-Jane Wilkins

Cataloging-in-Publication Data is available from
the Library of Congress

ISBN 978-1-62588-384-1

Photo acknowledgements
t = top, b = bottom, l = left, r = right, c = center
page 1 terekhov igor; 2t rickyd, b Christian Delbert; 3, 4 My Good
Images; 5t Jim David, b bikeriderlondon; 6 My Good Images;
7 Anton Gvozdikov; 8t to b My Good Images, OZaiachin,
zhangyang13576997233, marekuliasz; 9t to b TerraceStudio,
pukach, designelements, Broadpeak; 10t Blazej Lyjak, b Veniamin
Kraskov; 11t Marek CECH, bl photo25th, br Mark Herreid;
12 gorillaimages; 13l jeff Metzger, r Brian Goodman;
14 steve estvanik; 16 Anton Gvozdikov; 17 Mirec;
18 Dudarev Mikhail; 19t WOLF AVNI;
20 Warren Goldswain; 21l mountainpix,
r Kristian Bell; 22 Schubbel; 23l Sam
DCruz, r B Calkins1/all Shutterstock
Front cover: My Good Images/Shutterstock

DAD0063
022015
9 8 7 6 5 4 3 2 1

CONTENTS

FEEL THE THRILL

Think you have the skill, strength, and stamina to give hiking a go? If you like the idea of striding out into the wilderness on an epic endurance trek, then read on...

Take the challenge

Imagine exploring the most remote places on Earth, battling through dense jungle, trudging through treacherous snowdrifts, or scrambling up steep mountain paths. Hiking tests you to the limit!

EXTREME BUT TRUE One of the most famous hiking routes in the world is the Appalachian Trail, which runs down the East Coast of America. It's just over 2,175 miles (3,500 km) long and takes around 175 days to cover.

Hiking can take you on adventures through amazing landscapes.

THRILL SEEKER

George Meegan (Britain)

FEAT
Hiked 19,019 miles (30,608 km)
over 6½ years

WHERE AND WHEN
From the southern tip of
South America to the most
northern point in Alaska,
1977–1983

Tough stuff

Proper hiking isn't a stroll in the woods—it's a long, tough slog, often in extreme cold or heat, and in all kinds of severe weather. You must be physically fit, well-prepared for difficulties or dangers, and able to keep a clear head if disaster strikes.

You'll be tackling all kinds of tricky terrain, so pack well and be prepared for anything!

SHAPE UP

Before you set off on a hiking trip, you need to train so you can tackle steep hills and long distances without getting exhausted or injured.

Being fit and healthy lets you take on bigger challenges.

Warming up

First get your heart pumping and your muscles warmed up and ready for exercise. Start by jogging in place or skipping for 10 minutes, then try some of these simple stretches.

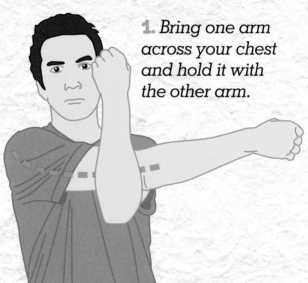

1. Bring one arm across your chest and hold it with the other arm.

2. Stand with feet apart, hands on hips. Swing hips around four times clockwise, then four times counterclockwise.

3. Take a big step forward and hold for three seconds, then step and hold with the other leg. Make four big strides; two with each leg.

Smart walking

Work on your walking technique to make sure you don't strain your body and use more effort than you need to. The more you walk, the fitter you'll get.

🦶 Take normal steps, not enormous strides.

🦶 Land on your heel and roll forward onto your toes before pushing up for the next step.

🦶 Push with your back leg, don't pull forward with your leading leg.

🦶 Swing your arms back and forth to propel you forward.

Joining a walking club is a great way to get fit and meet friends to hike with.

GET THE GEAR

Wearing the right clothes makes a difference in bad weather, and helps to keep you comfortable and safe. Here's what you need.

Layering up

Lots of thin layers are better than one or two thick ones. Start with thermals or a T-shirt, add a sweatshirt or fleece, and finish with a waterproof outer layer. Add more layers in cold weather. You can always peel them off.

A good-quality waterproof layer will keep rain out, but also let your skin breathe so you don't sweat too much.

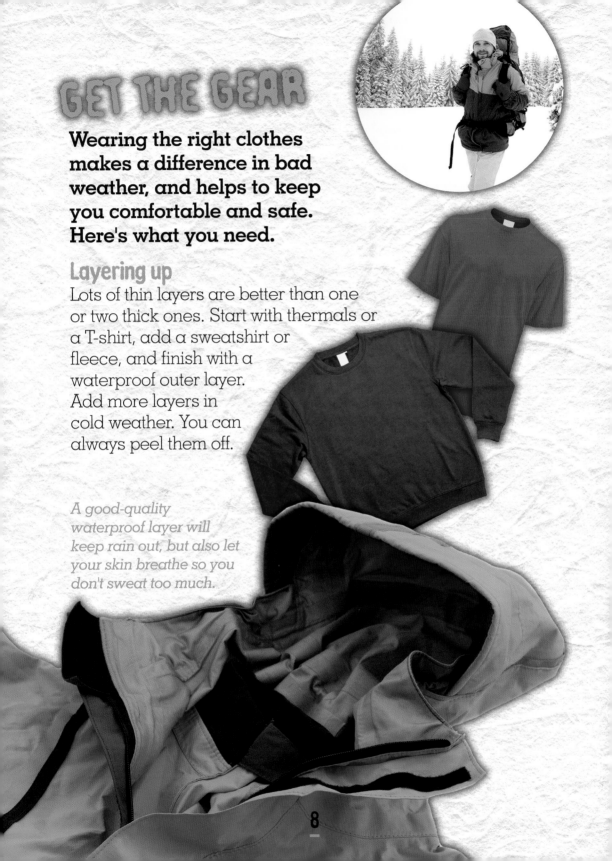

Essential extras

Don't forget a hat, gloves, and warm socks. Take spare clothes in case you're cold or you get wet. Remember to put on sunscreen when it's hot!

EXTREME BUT TRUE Leaving your nose, ears, or hands uncovered in extremely cold weather can lead to a painful condition called **frostbite**. If left untreated, fingers and toes may even drop off.

Good boots

Strong boots with good ankle support are vital. Wear new boots on short hikes first to break them in. It's no fun walking with sore and blistered feet!

SURVIVAL KITS

When you head off on a hiking adventure, you need supplies to last several days. Pack sensibly and make sure you can carry everything!

EXTREME BUT TRUE You can only survive for two or three days without water—so be sure to pack some!

Take a tent

The best tents are dome-shaped and stable in high winds, which is useful in mountains or exposed areas. They can be tricky to put up, so practice before you go.

Use side pockets for items you need regularly, such as a compass or water bottle

*A **dome tent** will keep you safe and dry in rain and high winds.*

Get cooking

You need a camping stove to cook food or boil water for a hot drink. Fuel is heavy, so think about how much you need. Take matches or a **steel and flint**, in case you need to make a camp fire.

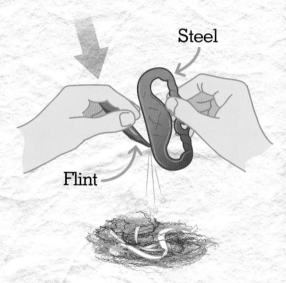

Steel

Flint

Gas stove plus fuel canister

Compact gas stove

Wash pots and pans after cooking, and never leave litter behind.

Useful gear

Other essentials include a sleeping pad and bag, food, water (plus **purification tablets**), and a first aid kit.

FINDING YOUR WAY

One vital hiking skill is planning a safe route and following it. A good trail avoids hazards such as crumbling cliffs and has camping spots along the way.

THRILL SEEKER

Jean-Louis Étienne (France)

FEAT
Hiked solo from northern Canada to North Pole in 63 days, using a radio transmitter for directions

WHERE AND WHEN
Canada, 1986

Reading a map

Never set out without a map! Know what the symbols mean and learn how to line it up with features you see around you to find where you are and which way you need to go.

Contour lines show the height of the land. The closer together they are, the more steeply the ground rises.

Use your compass with the map to work out which way you're facing and where you need to go.

Using a compass

A compass helps you work out which way you're facing. The red end of its magnetic arrow always points north and the other end south. Hold it level and let the arrow swing to north, then turn the dial so the "N" for north lines up with the needle.

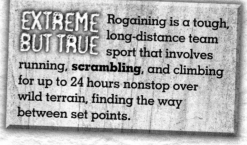

EXTREME BUT TRUE Rogaining is a tough, long-distance team sport that involves running, **scrambling**, and climbing for up to 24 hours nonstop over wild terrain, finding the way between set points.

HILL HIKING

Want to tackle a seriously tough hike? Try a hill or mountain climb—but train properly first, and don't take on anything too difficult.

As well as being steep, mountain hikes may follow narrow, crumbling paths.

EXTREME BUT TRUE The Colorado Trail is a dizzyingly high hike for experienced walkers only. It reaches a high point of just over 13,123 feet (4,000 m).

Watch out!

High places can be misty and rainy. The temperature will drop as you climb, and the wind will blow more strongly. Fog or blizzards may leave you lost and confused, while **avalanches** or rock slides can be fatal. Travel in a group, watch the weather forecast, and take survival gear.

Find shelter

Never hike through a storm. Stop and shelter in the safest place you can find: a cave, overhanging cliff, or even a hollow in the ground. In snow, find a deep drift and dig a hole big enough to crawl into.

Air hole

Entrance

1. Use a flat object to dig a hole in a snowdrift just big enough for you and your gear.

2. Poke air holes in the top and close the entrance with a block of snow or your backpack.

WILD WATER

You can follow a river if you're lost, but rivers can be dangerous too. Here are some tips to help you stay safe when hiking near water.

If you have to cross water, walk slowly and carefully. Rocks may be slippery.

River dangers

Rivers have strong **currents** that can sweep you off your feet. Always try to cross at a bridge, even if you have to go out of your way to find one. Avoid boggy, marshy banks where you could slip or sink into mud.

*In **quicksand**, lie flat to spread your weight so you don't sink. Slowly wriggle to dry land.*

Flood risks

Heavy rain can make water levels rise fast and turn streams into raging torrents. Don't camp or walk near swollen rivers that could burst their banks and flood. Find a new route or turn back.

EXTREME BUT TRUE

Flash floods are big, sudden floods that happen when something blocks a river, such as a landslide, forcing a huge amount of water to spill over the banks.

DESERT TREKS

Hiking across dry, dusty deserts is a real challenge. These are hostile places, so train hard and prepare well.

*There isn't much shelter in the desert, so pack a tent or **tarpaulin** to rig up at night.*

EXTREME BUT TRUE The highest desert temperature ever recorded is 136.4°F (58°C) in Libya, North Africa.

Hot and cold

Deserts can be blisteringly hot by day and bitterly cold at night. Walk in the early morning or evening and rest in shade during the hottest part of the day. Cover up with light, loose layers, and take extra clothing for nights.

Copy wild animals and find shade when the sun is blazing!

Water!

Water is essential. Your body loses water as you sweat and will soon become **dehydrated** if you don't keep drinking. Carry as much water as you can and look out for **water holes**.

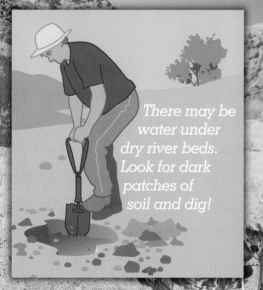

There may be water under dry river beds. Look for dark patches of soil and dig!

THRILL SEEKER

Mauro Prosperi (Italy)

FEAT
Survived 9 days in the desert after getting lost in a sandstorm; drank bat and snake blood until rescued

WHERE AND WHEN
Sahara Desert, Morocco, 1994

EMERGENCY!

Don't let your hike end in disaster—plan properly, travel with friends, and stay alert for danger.

Keep your head

If something goes wrong, don't panic. Keep calm and act fast to make sure things don't get worse. This means finding shelter, staying warm, and calling for help as soon as possible.

Learn basic first aid so you can treat minor injuries such as cuts, scrapes, and sprains.

THRILL SEEKER

Jamie Neale (Britain)

FEAT
Survived nearly two weeks after getting lost on a hike; crawled under logs at night until rescued

WHERE AND WHEN
Blue Mountains, Australia, 2009

Rescue services

Every year, mountain rescue services help hikers in trouble up in the hills. Teams of skilled rescuers use helicopters and even highly trained dogs to find injured or lost hikers.

Try to move into an open area so the rescue team can spot you easily and lift you to safety.

Remember!

Stick to hiking trails and paths so you avoid hazards such as disturbing wild animals in dens or deep undergrowth. You'll be less likely to get lost, too.

If a snake bites you, wash the bitten area and get help. Never cut skin to try to get rid of venom.

INDEX